native bott

Lean Analytics

The Ultimate Guide to an Agile Way of Analytics, Advanced Analytics, and Data Science for a Superior Way to Build Startups and Run Enterprises

Contents

Introduction

The following chapters discuss how to incorporate Lean Analytics into your startup company, and from there, how to use Lean Analytics to streamline your company and make it the best that it can be. In the process, Lean philosophy is also examined and all of the things that apply to it.

Conventional business philosophy falls short in many ways. This is partially because the conventional business strategy is from a time where available data wasn't nearly as great as it is now. Lean Analytics is a natural evolution in the approach to business – it represents a more streamlined business model in the information age.

This book provides everything you need to learn about this model and how you can use it to your advantage.

Chapter 1: Introduction to Lean Analytics

Lean Analytics is the engine which powers the concept of using Lean principles to guide your startup. It is an essential hallmark of the concept of *build-measure-learn*, which is discussed in the next section.

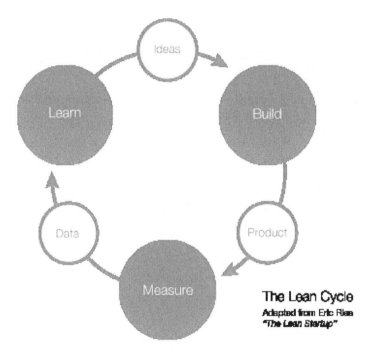

The Lean Cycle
Adapted from Eric Ries
"The Lean Startup"

To understand Lean Analytics, you also need to understand Lean itself.

Lean has its origin in the 1980s, with a concept known as *Lean manufacturing*. Lean manufacturing was a concept developed to help American production companies compete with Japanese production companies.

Essentially, Japanese production companies had their own methodology for trimming down the business cycle and production process and making things run far smoother than normal. American companies lagged behind and produced waste in comparison – waste being a relative term applying, of course, to more than just the trash that the company generates. Waste in the Lean conceptualization is the expense of anything that doesn't need to be expended, and in this capacity, you can start to form a wider idea of what *waste* can mean.

Money isn't your only expenditure – though it is, of course, one form. The process of starting a business and running a production process involves different resources, all of which can be wasted. Time, for example, is a resource as dead time means dead labor, which means that you are spending money on labor that isn't utilized. Moreover, time is also a resource because the market is constantly shifting and time wasted means that you aren't actively meeting a demand in the market at that given moment.

There are numerous resources which the Lean process aims to avoid wasting – time, the actual labor, the money spent on labor, the additional raw resources used in the process and ultimately wasted, and so forth. Perhaps the biggest waste is things produced in excess that isn't bought or things which oversaturate the market and don't fit a certain demand, as well as things which are processed beyond what the market requires. This doesn't include products which are defective because of an ineffective manufacturing process or something of a similar nature.

Lean, therefore, aims to ameliorate these problems and eliminate the waste from production processes through a standardized methodology of analyzing the waste and then making gradual, continual improvements to the company.

Down the line, sometime in the 2000s, came a concept called *Lean Startup*, which recognizes that there are many commonalities between the manufacturing process and the process of starting a company, with the first and greatest commonalities being that both require a constant resource pool and have the capacity to produce quite a bit of waste.

The Lean Startup model is benefited and carried along by the concept of Lean Analytics, which bolsters the concept and makes it run far smoother. Lean Startup recognized that in the process of starting a business, there is quite a bit of capital poured into it that can be wasted and general risk undertaken. The Lean Startup process intends to improve both of these issues by coming up with ways to reduce the overall amount of resources and time invested as well as the overall amount of risk accrued by the investor.

You may be wondering how this is the case. For that, the Lean Startup concept offers a vivid framework for developing a worthwhile startup, from the conception process to the actual development of your company. Even though this book isn't about Lean Startup per se, it is about one of the most powerful engines *for* Lean Startup. Thus, now you will learn about those concepts so that you know what you're getting into with all of it.

Lean Startup

The Lean Analytics method is tailored toward startups to help them mature and quickly become just what the world needs at the moment. The reality is that most startups don't start out with an explicit goal in mind, and their exact purpose will often change and mutate quite a bit over the course of the company's development. Indeed, a lot of the time, your first formulation of a company ends up being nothing like what the company turns out to be, even if it's successful. But there are also times when it does – there are instances when a company will turn out to be correct in its initial assessment. However, this doesn't discount the fact that many different companies *do* end up pivoting and shifting their resources elsewhere.

One of the key philosophies underlying Lean Startup, in general, is the idea that you shouldn't try to make the market adjust to your company – you're almost never going to be able to do that without extremely clever presentation and marketing, like Apple. However, a lot of the time, you *can* try to make your company fit the market. Doing so means that you're likely to save a lot of money that might otherwise be spent on extraneous business processes or end up wasted. And capital, for better or worse, is extremely important to the startup process; you need to be sure that you waste as little of those resources as possible. The capital that you might spend on a failing venture could instead be spent on expanding your company and vision down the line – if you were to follow a more effective methodology for figuring out the direction of your business instead.

In this capacity, Lean Startup encompasses several concepts aimed at ensuring that you can come up with a solid and worthwhile business idea from the very start, then build the company around that concept. That way, you'll have a firmer and more worthwhile business foundation going forward, as well as a greater chance of success on the general market.

Therefore, to understand better what purpose Lean Analytics serve, you're going to start by dissecting Lean Startup and getting a better idea of the underlying concepts. You're then going to work with Lean Analytics to integrate them into this process and help you build a better business from day one.

More on Lean Startup

Lean Startup is founded on the ideas already covered, i.e., that businesses tend to require a huge amount of both risk and capital upon starting and that this risk and capital can, therefore, be mitigated through worthwhile production techniques. Though it cannot be done entirely, the amount of overall risk and capital being put forth just for starting a company can be reduced many times over. As a result, the money saved can be used for reinvestment into the business, or it could stay in your pocketbook to give the business a longer life expectancy.

With any company, you are attempting to generate value. When working with a concept such as Lean Startup, it is actually through these concepts of value generation that one ought to be operating. You try to firstly eliminate as many wasteful practices as you reasonably can while also trying to build the amount of value that you generate through the processes within your company.

Understand first and foremost that the Lean Startup philosophy has almost nothing to do with how many resources you start out with nor with how much capital you have at your disposal; rather, Lean Startup has to do with the useful application of said resources and capital and how you can start from ground zero to start building up and making something that the market demands.

There are essentially two types of business owners. There are business owners who start with an idea and then attempt to act on it and bring it to market, and there are business owners who don't bring with them a set goal and rather only want to *own a business* and be their own boss. Neither kind of business owner is necessarily wrong in their approach, and both can be helped substantially by the concepts underlying the Lean Startup methodology.

Let's start with an exploration of these concepts, and later the focus will be on their application and integration with Lean Analytics methods.

The first major concept of Lean Startups is the concept of the *minimum viable product*. When you hear the term 'minimum viable product', you might end up confused about what the term implies. In many ways, however, it's quite self-explanatory. The minimum viable product is the most essential expression of your core business idea, one which you can release to get meaningful data. It isn't necessarily the finished or final version of your product or program;

a good example would be the alpha or even the pre-alpha release of a piece of software wherein core groups are allowed to test it out and give meaningful feedback about it.

This is an important part of Lean Startups, and the reason it's so important is because one of the most basic ideas behind Lean Startup methodology is that you must constantly be changing your product and your company to meet the changing market's demands. As mentioned earlier, your goal isn't necessarily to make the market want your product – your goal is to make the product that the market wants.

So the Lean methodology is about doing just that: releasing things in incremental versions, firstly so that you can rapidly get feedback about different aspects, and secondly so that you could avoid investing too much on a given part in case you need to change course in some major way. The idea of a minimum viable product intertwines deeply with this because when you release a minimum viable product to a target group, you're able to quickly and efficiently receive information and feedback from the said target group and then make the necessary changes in response. If the target group particularly likes or dislikes something about the product, or if the group makes a request or suggestion, you can rapidly and dynamically make adjustments or modifications to the product in response to the user statements, without having lost a significant amount of capital in the process.

Understanding this is critical to understanding both the Lean Startup process and the utility of Lean Analytics itself. You need to recognize that the whole point is essentially staying light on your feet without investing far too much into any singular idea until you know that an investment in that particular idea is the right way to go. For this reason, there is another fundamental Lean Startup concept that you need to understand: the *pivot*.

Pivots are a little more complex and difficult to understand at first glance. However, they're relatively intuitive. A pivot is a backup plan or an alternative way of using the same resources on your hand for a *secondary* business idea. That is, if your first venture doesn't pan out, you should be able to employ the resources for that first venture for your pivot, which could end up having better applicability and acceptance on the market than your initial idea. There are numerous examples of pivots that have been employed in technology and business in general, where companies have shifted away from their original ideas and business plans to move toward a more profitable idea. The essential philosophy behind the pivot is the notion of changing courses without changing the people navigating.

So, bearing all of this in mind, what role does Lean Analytics specifically play? Well, as mentioned, one of the difficulties of running a business is that you have a limited amount of currency to work with. The chief goal of Lean Analytics is to help you fit in with the market in a meaningful way through a product or service that people actually want – before your initial capital pool starts to run out.

Data Informed vs. Data Driven

In running a company based off of Lean Startup and Lean Analytics principles, it's important that you understand a central distinction between things being *data informed* and things being *data-driven*. There is a lot to understand about this distinction, so let's break it down and explore it.

Data-informed and *data-driven* companies have a very different philosophy at their core. Where *data-informed* companies place more emphasis on the simple usage of data to make more informed decisions regarding the company and how it's run, *data-driven* companies instead use data at their very core and use it to form almost *every* decision.

The purpose of Lean Analytics is to make heavy use of data to drive your company forward and help you learn everything there is to learn to accomplish it. It's also used to identify key metrics that can aid in your goal. Metrics, of course, are measured data used to influence decisions at a later point.

Metrics

Perhaps the hardest part of learning about Lean Analytics is learning what metrics are important to your young company. With time, however, it will become easier. This book is going to explore what metrics are most important to you and your company and what things you need to pay attention to most when trying to build up a data-driven model.

Let's start with an exploration of what metrics are.

Metrics are essentially any sort of data that you gather through analytic methods, and that correlates to your product or service in one way or another. Metrics are normally divided into one of two types: *actionable metrics* and *vanity metrics*.

Actionable metrics are metrics that can be used to make solid decisions regarding your business and that give an honest picture of how the business in question is performing. These are the things that you want to look out for, and once explored a bit more in-depth, you'll learn about what kind of things might be considered actionable metrics.

Vanity metrics, on the other hand, are just metrics that you use to make your business look or sound good. However, you shouldn't use them to make decisions because they have little bearing on how your company actually functions and operates. These are things that you might bring up to outsiders but most certainly won't want to use as a measure for how your company is running.

Why Metrics?

Many people find data tedious and boring; however, the reality is that data isn't boring. Data is just reality being collected – or reality being manipulated. In either case, it gives you extremely valuable information about what you need to do, why, and how.

Perhaps that's the most useful part of data; when you heavily integrate data into your mode of business, what you're essentially doing is saying to yourself, "Okay, this is going to be an honest system." You're telling yourself that you're going to focus on hard numbers and use those to make decisions – instead of things like gut instincts or contextual variances which may lead you astray (e.g., having a lot of customers enter a shop doesn't matter if none of them buys anything; traffic in itself doesn't matter, the data *related* to this traffic is what matters).

When you work with data, you start to learn about how the numeric aspect of business really works and how you can use and manipulate the numbers to your advantage. This navigation of a given set of data can give you all of the information you need to push your business ahead of the competition.

However, to work with this data, you need a firm groundwork, and that's what this book is trying to build. Let's spend a little time talking about the process of starting a business using the Lean Startup technique. Afterward, how Lean Analytics can fit into the equation will then be discussed.

Chapter 2: Building a Startup Identity

In starting to understand the how and why of Lean Analytics, and generally using alternative methods of business building against the traditional mainstream model of business building (i.e., get an investment, make a product, succeed or fail), let's start with the story of the penny machine.

The story of the penny machine is commonly used to tell people how investors think and what investors want to see, but investors also use it to get the executives of new startup companies to start thinking like people who want to make money. You can also benefit from it by learning how to get people to think about your promising startup in general. The thing is, there are certain phrases that people who are potentially interested in your startup want to hear, and knowing what those phrases are and how to entice those people is key to having a meaningful business experience when you're just starting out.

But on to the story. It's midsummer in Palo Alto, and in a big room like an auditorium, there is a lit stage. People are seated, anxious to see what the person set to perform is going to do. Suddenly, in walks a man in a suit, carrying a large box. He walks to the stage, steps up onto it, and places the box on the floor, next to a stool that had been sitting in the middle. He adjusts his tie then opens the box. He pulls out a machine that looks similar to those found in arcades and grocery stores – the ones where you insert a coin into a slot to get some cheap knick-knack – and places it carefully on the stool.

He then asks if anybody nearby has a penny to spare, and nervously, a young man who was helping with the presentations that day hands him a penny. The man pops the penny into the machine. He pulls a lever, and the coin tumbles down. Out pops a nickel, shiny and clean.

The audience is confused.

One man pipes up, "All right, that's a neat trick."

In response, the man puts another penny in – and out comes another nickel, just as shiny and clean as the one before it. The audience *oohs* and *ahs*, obviously confused, and the man does the same thing with a nickel, putting the nickel into the machine which would return a dime.

That same investor speaks up again, "That's all well and good, but how does it work?"

Hearing this, the man with the machine laughs under his breath and pulls the machine open. The audience, who expected to see bags or slots of coins inside, were instead greeted with nothing of the sort – just a bunch of machinery, glimmering and shining and clean, none of it particularly large enough to be holding a stockpile of infinite coins.

That same investor speaks yet again: "That's very neat. Just one more question, and I think you and I may be able to cut a deal. What's keeping somebody else from doing it?"

The man smirks and replies, "I am the sole owner of the intellectual property of this machine, and I am the only one legally allowed by the U.S. government to mint new coins."

Now, this story clearly never happened in reality – such a magical money machine can't exist. But you can pretty easily see the point.

There are things that investors want to hear. There is nothing that is more of a goldmine to a potential investor than something that is, in one manner of speaking or another, a literal penny machine that they can put money into and have money spat back at them tenfold.

This is important to bear in mind going forward. In this chapter, the process of actually *starting* a startup, as well as integrating Lean Analytics into it from the very beginning, will be discussed. However, for you to excel at this particular lesson, there are some things that you need to understand from the very beginning.

Perhaps the most compelling and important lesson is that a business is not a feel-good entity. You are not doing this to fulfill one dream or another. If you have a dream of pushing a product to market and making the market want it, then you are going to quickly realize that such a thing is only a fantasy, and an ill-advised fantasy at that.

With that said, though, if you can change your mindset just a little bit and focus on the business aspect rather than on just the product aspect, you're going to find yourself excelling in whatever field you aim to go into and with whatever product that you aim to introduce.

It's worth noting at this point that this specific method for starting a business is perhaps best tailored to the Internet and Internet-based startups because the necessary analytic tools are already there for you in many ways. In addition, when everything occurs on the Internet, it's easier to gather a lot more data than you might be able to otherwise. Furthermore, when you're working with a business that's based on the Internet, or even on an Internet tech startup, you have a lot more opportunity to make money through other avenues, particularly through smart advertising.

Perhaps the best reason that the Lean Startup methodology works best for online businesses is because of the immediacy and of the relatively lower capital needed. To start a business on the ground, you'll first have to hope that the target market in your area is sufficiently large for your product to be useful. Secondly, instead of simply fitting their needs, you're going to have to hope that the market in your area actually *likes* your product. Beyond all of this, you're also going to have to pay standing capital to rent a location, and then you're going to have to pay for any additional fees, such as a business license. Going this route simply isn't practical, and it's something you really ought to avoid if it's at all possible.

Compare this instead to starting an Internet-based company. Firstly, all you're really paying for is the domain and whatever other services you end up using, meaning you don't have to pay for standing capital and so forth. Furthermore, when you have a shipping-based business – if that is one of the things you end up aiming for – you don't particularly need to keep your inventory *in stock* and can instead act as a middleman or a drop-shipper, acting in between a manufacturer or wholesaler and the final consumer of your goods, meaning that you don't have to spend money to stock inventory either.

To this extent, there are a lot of business ideas and formulations that actually go fairly well with the concept of an online business, such as affiliate marketing and so forth. Having easy access to these sorts of things makes it extremely easy to expand your business and make additional profit. Moreover, as I said before, the metrics that are available to you when you run an online business are profoundly better than what you could get otherwise, simply because the Internet is entirely data-based whereas a physical business requires you to convert things into data that you can manipulate and analyze.

With the latter, you don't get important statistics such as click-through rate or impressions. Moreover, when your business is conducted via the Internet, you also easily gain the ability to expand your business into other internet-based services. For example, when you have an Internet-based business, it's extremely simple to integrate social media into it – and this can make quite a difference. Social media makes it easy for people to "share" with others the things and services that they like, and you want to make sure that your business is one of those things that they like! It tends to be more difficult to integrate this same experience with a standing business.

So, with all of that in mind, let's now start talking about the very foundations of starting a business and integrating Lean Analytics into its very core. This should make it easy for you to build on top of these ideas and start working with them in an essential way.

Foundations

Every startup concept starts somewhere. Imagine it as though you're building the foundations to a house. You want to build the strongest base possible so that the house can be built quickly and can stand the test of time. Not all startup ideas are good and realizing this is an important part of the process.

In assessing what kind of startup ideas are valuable, it's important to start by analyzing what is *needed* rather than what is *wanted*. It is particularly difficult to make the market fit to what you think it should be; far more difficult, in fact, than trying to make your product or offering fit the market. I know I've already said this a couple of times, but it really cannot be stressed enough. Your business will only be as successful as you're willing to allow it to be.

This all plays into an essential concept known as growth hacking. Repeat businessmen realize that there *is* a way to make a business succeed, and it isn't just to throw money at it until it starts to work in your favor. In fact, getting the money for a business is only half the battle, and money thrown at a bad or derivative idea isn't going to get you anywhere particularly.

Just take a look at NeXT Computing. NeXT was a venture launched by Steve Jobs after he was ousted from Apple. He put an extremely large amount of money into trying to get NeXT off the ground, to little avail. The computers were ugly, the hardware unimpressive, the price tag steep, and the practicality low. There were simply very few reasons for universities and businesses to choose NeXT computers over standing technological giants such as IBM and Apple. An excessive amount of money was put into trying to make NeXT work, but ultimately, NeXT ended up being a failure.

Numerous different case studies can be done on companies that started with an idea that simply didn't have a market and that then shifted course, the "pivot" that we talked about earlier. Later on, pivots and how to implement the technique effectively will be examined more in-depth. However, for the moment, you only need to understand this core lesson: not every business idea is going to go over well.

Recognize and understand this. Unless the idea is truly revolutionary in one way or another, is profitable, and/or is approachable, there are few instances wherein you ought to start a business solely because you have what *you* think is a good idea. In all other cases, there simply isn't going to be much appeal on the market for your idea. An example of this would be the Oculus Rift virtual reality headset. While it was novel and innovative, it spared no money, and more importantly, no time appealing to a brand-new market. It was truly innovative, and a bit more startup capital was both necessary and understandable for such a product because the idea was clearly good and marketable. This was bolstered by a large Kickstarter campaign which affirmed the fact that there was indeed a user-base that found the idea of virtual reality implementations for common hardware to be particularly cool. The entire thing came about as a result of the initial investor's long-time interest in the concepts underlying virtual reality. As a result, a capital investment into such a novel idea would have been safe.

Perhaps Bitcoin could be yet another example of a technology that was novel and innovative. However, the difference between Bitcoin and the Oculus Rift is that where the Oculus Rift required a place for manufacturing to occur, the development of Bitcoin cost next to nothing. Bitcoin, coming into unexpected popularity, would end up making the original developer a billionaire – and a billionaire in secrecy.

So, what can we learn from these two cases specifically? The fact is, novel ideas can be good and worthwhile. But in the first case, the market was confirmed to be there, and in the second case, the initial development didn't cost anything. If Bitcoin *didn't* become popular, then the developers wouldn't have taken a loss at all.

However, what if two things happened? What if, first and foremost, Bitcoin *hadn't* become successful? And, more importantly, what if on top of it not becoming successful, Bitcoin required *capital investment*? Bitcoin would have taken a loss in this case, despite being innovative.

The lesson here is not to decry innovation. No, not at all. Rather, it's to make the point that to be an effective entrepreneur you need to have a firm sense of not just what can be changed for the better but also what people *want* to be changed for the better. Unfortunately, the nature of the market and of starting a business makes it difficult to tell what people want or will buy until you actually dip your toes in the water and test out a product. This is where the Lean method comes in.

Through a combination of the Lean Startup methodology and the Lean Analytics framework, you're going to be working lightly and with rich ideas so that you can make meaningful changes to your business paradigm as time goes on. And all of this starts with a central idea.

So then, how does one come up with an idea for a business? That's a more difficult question to answer, but we're going to try to anyway. Sometimes "bad" business ideas succeed, and sometimes "good" business ideas fail. A lot of the time, investors and entrepreneurs only have the specific way that they see and understand the market to work with, and this doesn't necessarily bode well.

Understand that a solid business idea means a profitable business idea. A good business idea isn't just one which floats along but rather one which has the potential to generate a huge amount of income for everybody involved. Look around for inspiration. Think about daily functions that you take part in, even if they're a little mundane. Consider something like Groupon. Groupon is simple conceptually, and it's one of those pivot businesses talked a lot about, where a business starts out with a different idea than what it ends up with. Essentially, Groupon is coupon-sharing service. It is incredibly simple, but it's also incredibly useful. Moreover, it's incredibly lucrative to the people who started it in the first place.

The lesson here is that inspiration can come from any number of places. But your best bet is to come up with an idea which either has little resource investment to start with or resources which, if you must invest in them, can easily be used in other business ideas as well. Not every idea is going to be smart, but some are, and these are the ideas that you most want to latch onto.

When you finally do hatch your business idea, you'll next need to start with a plan. There are numerous reasons for why you really ought to have your business laid out on paper before you ever do anything else with it. Perhaps the most useful and most worth considering is the fact that when you have a startup, it's incredibly easy to lose focus. This will be discussed more later on, but it's a simple truth. When you're in command of a startup, it's really hard to keep your eyes on the prize at all times. You just might lose sight of your goals and objectives very easily. In a way, integrating Lean Analytics will also help you to keep focus on all of your goals going forward as you start to really understand the flow of owning a business and start presenting a better and better product. The specific way in which analytics will help you to maintain focus will be examined later on when the discussion turns to those concepts specifically.

Perhaps the best way to start figuring out an actionable business plan is by using the Lean Canvas. You can Google it and gain easy access; it's free and easy to use. But what is it? To understand the Lean Canvas, you first need to understand the Business Model Canvas.

The Business Model Canvas is a method by which you can figure out important information about your company and lay out its activities, as well as a bunch of more finite information, to have it all in one place. Doing so will help you more easily visualize what things need to be changed and what things can stay the same.

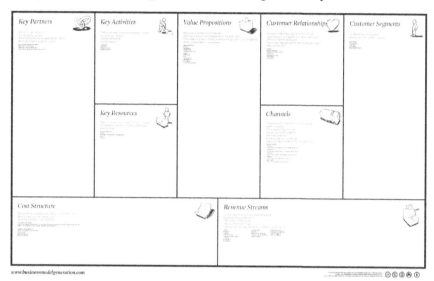

The Lean Canvas, on the other hand, is an adaptation of this model, which is primarily geared at new startup companies. Essentially what the Lean Canvas does is to allow you to specifically focus on addressing problems that you intend to solve with your given product. It gives you a framework and a simple template through which you can work on addressing said problems.

This is great because working with a simpler framework like the Lean Canvas is by far preferable in many ways to the traditional approach of incredibly long business plans and the like. Why work on some twenty-five-page document detailing the long-term goals and plans of your business when it isn't necessary? Using the Lean Canvas, you can get all of the important ideas out there, digestible in a page or less. Afterward, you can easily share it with all of your friends and potential business partners at no cost. Don't forget that you can also create as many of these as you want on the site for free. The Lean Canvas is intended to streamline the very start of your business by helping you figure out your idea and come up with some sort of game plan for it.

During the development of your business plan, remember that you're trying to fill a market and try to make your overall goal with your business be as approachable as possible. Don't forget – regardless of how you're getting your startup capital you want your idea to sound like the penny machine we talked about earlier. Moreover, you want it to *be* a penny machine. Building a penny machine idea centers on your long-term business plan, and much of the ideas of Lean Startup revolve around it.

Chapter 3: The Lean Approach to Startups

This chapter digs into the specifics of how the Lean approach is different and how the concept of Lean Analytics integrates into the startup approach.

As previously mentioned, there are quite a few things that are components to this. However, it's important that before anything else, a chapter is spent on going over the philosophy of the business idea and figuring out what constitutes a "good" business idea. This has just been examined, and it should've given you invaluable guidance going forward on what ideas to implement in your startup, and how. Let's add a little bit more to what's been covered and start talking about how the actual running of your company is supposed to work, with an emphasis on Lean Analytics as well.

Let's imagine that you've picked out a business idea. You know what you want to do and what to work on, and you're ready to start moving forward with your company. Or maybe you're not quite there yet, and you just want some ideas about how the Lean Analytics process works before you invest a lot into this framework. Perhaps you first want to learn some sort of process.

Whatever the case, it's important that you have a firm idea of how a data-driven approach differs from a data-informed approach. At the very core of the business, as well as the approaches, are some fundamental differences that provide an obvious delineation between the two.

With traditional businesses, a lot of time and thought is invested into the company, with a significant amount of stock put forward on elaborate plans and predictions which might or might not pan out just as you're intending. Lean Startups, especially when facilitated by Lean Analytics, don't have this. Rather, they focus quite a bit on speed, i.e., on getting an idea out as fast as possible, then iterating on that idea based on feedback and metrics.

Knowing the distinction between Lean Startups and traditional startups is vital if you want to be a productive entrepreneur. When you're working with a Lean Startup, your focus is on putting something out and then making it adjust to fit the market, offering yourself the opportunity to change course if you need to. In this capacity, Lean Startups focus heavily on working lightly. Don't pour too much capital or time into something that you're not sure will work, and especially make sure always to give yourself a backup plan and have enough capital left over to pivot if necessary.

As mentioned, Lean Startups place a lot of emphasis on metrics, and Lean Analytics is all about having a systematic manner by which you can actually analyze these metrics and glean useful information. Certain metrics can give you a whole lot of information. To gain a better understanding of Lean Analytics, it's important that you know the cycle of the data-driven startup: Build-Measure-Learn.

Build-Measure-Learn

At this point, you've gotten some sort of identity and barebones plan for your startup. You've also received an idea for a minimum viable product, and you probably want to move on from this and finally start working toward some meaningful practice and hopefully making some money along the way.

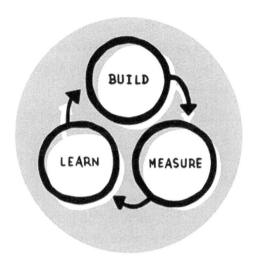

It's time to discuss the concept of metrics and build-measure-learn. Build-measure-learn itself is one of the fundamental concepts of startups that you need to understand. It's an inherent cycle that takes place within every startup, and Lean Startups emphasize this in particular. It's important that you understand all of this stuff about Lean Startups because it can really help you set the scene for what Lean Analytics are and why you need to understand them, as well as how they integrate.

So what is build-measure-learn? Build-measure-learn describes the three essential processes of any business. You start with an *idea*. Ideas are things that you can build on to push your product forward or try to make some sort of impact on the market. These are any adjustments or new products that you might put on the market. You then *build* these ideas that you see as good. This encapsulates the build part of the loop.

After you build it, you have a product on your hands. You can use this product in multiple ways, either pushing it to market, doing experiments with a segment of your overall market or keeping your product in a perpetual update loop for *all* consumers. There are many different ways to approach this in particular, but this is where analytics start to become important. Analytics offers you the ability to perform the *measure* part of the loop. It is at this point that you start to learn how people respond to the changes made to your product and what changes you should or shouldn't have made, as well as how you can and should adjust your product in the future to make it fit better with your target markets.

After you measure, you're going to have *data*. This data is the pillar of the whole process because it allows you to make informed decisions about the products you build and the changes you make to these products. This process is known as *learning*. Learning takes place whenever you use data to make informed decisions about products based on customer responses. You then use that to make your business flow more smoothly and make better profit margins, which is ultimately the end goal.

With the data, you have two options – *pivot* or *persevere*. Pivoting is deciding to shift away from your core business idea or a particular change to your product or business after analyzing people's response to it. This is the beauty of the Lean analytical approach – it allows you to act dynamically. And though the process is responsive, it is a *quick* kind of responsivity that allows you to make meaningful decisions regarding your data without investing too much capital into it and without ostracizing your user base by rolling out massive changes that you might not be comfortable about, to begin with.

One way or another, this process specifically will give you *ideas*. It is rather clear that this is the point at which the loop starts over yet again, and you're now ready to move on to the next part of the loop, the build process.

This is a brilliant model because it allows you to make informed decisions about your customers. Other businesses following a traditional model may not take the time to get customer input, and as a result, they may pour a lot of capital and resources into a change or a product that very few people are interested in. This, of course, is not quite ideal! You'll end up wasting many resources that you really didn't have to waste, just because of your inability to take a moment and utilize a more incremental process.

This then raises the question of how one moves forward with a Lean Analytics approach. How exactly does the measure process take place, and how does the data from the measure process inform the learning process? This is the focus of the rest of this book now that we've properly set the stage for it by analyzing Lean Startup and its various utilities.

All of this analysis takes place using metrics. We previously defined metrics in brief in this book, but they're essentially any gathered and measured information regarding your users that you can use to make decisions. This is easy enough to say, but it leaves you wondering: how will I know what metrics are important to me?

That is a harder question to answer. It revolves, partly, around knowing what kind of business model you're following and what stage your company is at. These two concepts build up what is known as the Lean Analytics framework.

The Lean Analytics Framework

The Lean Analytics framework, as previously stated, is based largely around knowing what stage your company is at and what type of company you have. Let's talk a little bit about what both of these terms mean, as well as how they may be seen. It is through these terms that you're going to build an idea of what metrics are important to your company.

Firstly, you have six different essential types of businesses that the Lean Analytics framework is geared toward. All of these are online businesses with different core purposes.

The first one is eCommerce. An eCommerce business is focused on the idea of managing and promoting an online storefront. eCommerce can constitute everything from Amazon to the online website for Shoe Locker or JCPenney, or even small no-name sites that you haven't heard of before. Basically, if something is being sold online, the site is eCommerce.

The second one is SaaS, commonly known as Software as a Service. This basically extends to any sort of software that companies host on their own computers that clients will then connect via the Internet to use. An example of this might be Google Apps, which people can use to fulfill various different purposes.

The third one is the mobile app, generally with a focus on free mobile apps. These are pretty self-explanatory; the concept of a free mobile app refers to any mobile app which is offered for free and for which the key way to make money is through revenue generated within the app itself, either through sales, microtransactions, or advertising.

The fourth is media. Media applies to anything that hosts entertainment or educational content, such as a website for a newspaper. These are also relatively easy to understand.

The fifth is user-generated content. User-generated content models are essentially sites where the primary content is developed and uploaded by the users of the sites themselves. This can be something such as YouTube or Medium.

The sixth and final type is the two-sided marketplace, which basically allows users to buy and list items for sale. This has different focuses from the eCommerce site because the users themselves are supplying the commerce on the site and it's not necessarily up to you to make the right calls on the site's inventory.

As you can see, all of these might have different things which are important to them independently, and all of them have different mechanisms by which they can generate revenue and make money. This will be discussed more in the chapter concerning revenue.

All of these businesses exist in five stages: empathy, stickiness, virality, revenue, and scale. Let's spend a minute or two discussing all five of these stages and what each of them implies for a business in each given archetype.

Stage

The five stages
EMPATHY
STICKINESS
VIRALITY
REVENUE
SCALE

The first stage is *empathy*. Empathy refers to the identification of a need in a given marketplace and then coming up with an idea that answers that need. All types of businesses go through this phase essentially, and it's not unique to any of the six business archetypes. At this particular point, one of the hardest tasks is getting people to visit your site in the first place.

The second stage is *stickiness*. In the stickiness stage, you're trying to focus on getting users to use and stay on your site. The most important thing at this point is generally having some sort of base that gets people to return. For eCommerce sites, the most important things would be paying attention to how loyal customers are and how many page conversions you're getting. For a two-sided market, a good metric for stickiness is how much inventory is actually being posted on the site. For a SaaS site, you really want to pay attention to how many people are using the service and – more importantly – how many people quit using the service after a couple of weeks, a phenomenon known as *churn*. For a mobile app, you can actually measure stickiness through the number of downloads for the app and how many users quit using the app. For the stickiness phase of a user-generated content site, you're trying to get as many people as possible to post content so that other users can enjoy the said content, but you're also trying to reduce the amount of spam posted on the site as much as possible. For media sites during the stickiness phase, you measure how many people visit your site and how many people come *back* to your site. You want to focus on getting as many return users as possible.

The third stage is *virality*. During the virality stage, your main focus is getting as many people as possible to visit your site and then trying to convert them into users. In essence, you're trying to increase the number of people who are coming to your site overall. Putting this after the stickiness phase allows you to get in place things that make people want to stay before you try attracting new people to the site in the first place. This means that more of your new users will be user conversions – a very good thing! Basically, you want users to tell their friends about the service you're offering, either because it's useful to them or intrinsic to something they do, or because you've incentivized them to do so through reward programs. In an eCommerce business model, for the virality stage, you're trying to get more people to share the site because of things they find useful. In a two-sided market, you're doing the same – you're hoping that people are going to share it in an attempt to display the things they're selling on the marketplace. SaaS has inherent virality because it's intrinsically useful and because when other people use it, they can share files or sometimes work together on common projects. This encourages people to use what their friends use. In mobile apps, you're attempting to get people to spread the game by word-of-mouth while also trying to get them to rate the app. Apps with higher and more ratings work to get more people to use your app because they'll see that it's good and that many people think so. User-generated content is normally shared in the virality phase through the sharing of the content that is posted in it, as well as through invites to the service in general. Media in the virality phase is spread through the virality of the content on the service.

The fourth stage is *revenue*. An entire chapter is devoted to this later on because it's such a dense topic, but essentially, revenue refers to the phase where you're trying to generate money off of the people that you've gained in the virality section.

The fifth stage is *scale*. You'll have found many bounds and good metrics in the previous phases and will have fine-tuned your business up to this point. Now, you're going to increase the overall size of operations. For the eCommerce business, you're going to want to do this through establishing affiliates for your products who can sell the product for you and generate money doing so, allowing you to distribute your products to a wider audience. For the two-sided market, you'll want to get people sharing your site as much as possible amongst their friends. For the SaaS business models, you can extend your scale by either implementing marketplaces within your product that give people access to more things, by offering access to your software on *other* marketplaces, or by letting people easily implement your software solutions through the development of an API that connects to your service. For a mobile app, you're going to want to develop applications similar to the ones that you've already developed to get people to check them out, and you're also going to want to get in contact with large publishing companies who will publish your app under their banner and get you more attention. For user-generated content, you can actually increase the scale of your operations by reselling the data that you get from the users on your site, which will net you a lot of profit and also enable you to keep up your operations through the capital gained. In media, you want to broaden the number of people who see your services through syndicating it to other channels and other media websites, as well as licensing the media that you create out to people.

Those are the five stages. Knowing that there are five different stages will help you understand what metrics you need to be chasing at any given time. Also note that these stages don't happen necessarily in order, and they can all be given different emphasis at different times. Businesses grow organically, and the stage that they're in at any given moment will shift in an equally organic manner, which can make it difficult to determine exactly what stage your business is in. However, a lot of the time, it will be obvious and will follow this pattern pretty organically. Note too that these things happen *cyclically*; you don't grow to the fifth stage, scale, then suddenly never have to work on your stickiness or your virality again. You will always be constantly improving and innovating as a business and trying to bolster your overall revenue and cash flow. This is part of the nature of the beast.

Chapter 4: Lean Analytics and the Measure Phase

In this chapter, metrics are discussed further. Though what a metric is has been defined, as well as the role that metrics play in building a Lean Startup, it's important to expand on this because it's intrinsically important to the entire topic. Along the way, the importance of building up the One Metric that Matters – yet another central concept to Lean Analytics – will also be examined.

Firstly, a lot of the analytics and metrics referred to from here on out can be tracked just by using the simple Google Analytics tool. This particular tool is recommended because it gives you a lot of useful insights into your company and how it's running without breaking the bank. There are also enterprise solutions if you grow sufficiently. Definitely conduct further research into Google Analytics and set your company up with it and similar solutions.

As mentioned, there are two different key types of metrics: the vanity and the actionable. However, they can also be divided into two different categories, namely qualitative and quantitative. The difference between quantitative and qualitative metrics is imperative to your company.

Essentially, qualitative metrics are metrics which aren't derived from numbers but can still be important to the interpretation of the numbers. For example, if you do customer surveys and you leave a response box at the bottom asking for feedback, you are receiving qualitative data through that response box, and this response box feedback can actually give you insight into the user's other responses on the form. Have you ever seen a Yelp review online where the user rates everything high but the overall score is low, and then in their review, they say something that they generally didn't like about the company, but everything else about it was great? This is a case where the raw numbers and data of the review wouldn't inform the company very much, but the review would inform the company as to how they could be making changes to the overall approach, i.e., regarding something that wasn't measurable within the other parts of the review.

This can be a big help to many companies, because many companies succeed at making what they aim to make – as in, the general quality of the product is good – but fail in ways that are hard to quantify specifically. For example, if you have an easy time drawing people into something, your quantitative metrics might be high. However, your quantitative metrics may also reveal that most people don't actually return, revealed through a low number of return visits from the same IP addresses, or low amounts of user activity a week after registration. The qualitative data that you uncover through surveys and opinion boxes will allow you to understand better why this is happening.

Surveys and opinion boxes, of course, are not the only way. Some companies will outsource their product or website to sites that distribute them amongst multiple users to conduct user-experience testing and receive feedback. More still might personally seek out repeat customers of the site to get customer interviews to understand better how customers feel about recent changes within the company and what ought to be changed. Qualitative metrics can be immensely significant overall to the direction of the company and can be a big revelation as to what customers actually think.

Quantitative metrics, on the other hand, are those metrics which have a bigger emphasis on numbers, as well as what can be expressed *through* those numbers. These could be many different things. It could be, for example, the monthly visitors to your site, the number of social media interactions, and so forth. These sorts of numbers can give you the ability to ask important questions about your data that you might not be asking in the first place, so it's of the utmost importance that you realize what quantitative metrics are as well as the role they play. Looking at quantitative metrics could give you interesting and important insight into how many people are using your service, how many people are buying your product, and how many people drop their subscription, among other things.

However, in noting all of this, it's important that you realize that not all metrics are good and not all metrics are bad. It's easy to define a good metric for analytics by breaking it down into four categories.

Firstly, you must be able to *compare* a metric. As in, you should be able to look at metrics over time and compare how they grow or change. This will give you insight into the shifting of the ratio and allow you to compare it to qualitative metrics and recent changes to your product to give you some idea of where something went wrong – or whether you're doing something right.

The metric must also be *easily understood*, especially if you are working on a team with other people. The entire team should understand a good metric, and everybody should know what that metric refers to, as well as what it symbolizes in the grand scheme of the company.

The best metrics are also *either ratios or rates.* While raw numbers can give you some sort of idea on the general scope of your company, they fail to give you meaningful insight into how people are acting. For example, simply looking at how many people have registered for your site doesn't really mean much. Sure, you may have a lot of registered users, but if most of those users never actually use the site and thereby don't generate revenue or contribute to growth, then the amount doesn't really matter. What's more important is what percentage of those users is actually *using* the site given a certain period, usually measured by the day but sometimes by the week.

Lastly, the measure should be able to *make an impact* on your behavior. If the metric changes, but the change doesn't actually mean anything or give you any information in the context of the company or how you can react, then the metric is pretty much worthless to you and should be ignored.

It's incredibly easy in the process of analytics to try to look at far too many metrics at once. Earlier in the book, we discussed briefly how many startup entrepreneurs absolutely lack a sense of focus. Lean Analytics, if you don't do it intelligently, isn't going to help you with this. In fact, it might hinder you if you don't do it right because you could easily become preoccupied with all of the metrics. It could render you unable to make meaningful decisions or shifts in your company because you can't tell what correlates to what.

It's important that you figure out what metrics are good and worthwhile and what metrics are bad so that you can weed out the things you can't be distracted by. Additionally, it's important early on that you start to place some emphasis on sticking to a singular metric and then trying to incite some sort of change to that metric in particular. However, before that is discussed, correlation and causation will be examined.

Correlation and Causation

In studying metrics, you'll come upon two relatively easy topics of discussion, correlation, and causation. While simple, they play a large part in the discussion of metrics and can actually be quite intrinsically difficult to deduce from an end-user's standpoint.

The lesson of correlation and causation is central. Two pieces of data may easily be correlated, without one causing the other. Being able to differentiate between the two and apply that differentiation to your metrics is paramount.

Two metrics may be correlated if they rise or fall in conjunction with one another. Two metrics are causal if one directly impacts or causes change to another metric. This is an important distinction because many people will look at two correlated metrics but will draw a causal link between them that doesn't quite exist.

If two things do move in a correlated manner, it could be because there is some sort of causal link between them. It could also be because they are both related to something else that's changing. However, there is also the chance that the two metrics are completely and entirely unrelated.

The example which is always used in this discussion is the connection between ice cream and drowning. A person may notice that at one point in their data, the rate at which people consumed ice cream went up. At that same point, the number of drowning went up. These two pieces of data are essentially correlated, of course, because they went up at the same time. The person may incorrectly conclude, however, that people who eat ice cream are more likely to drown; it is simply the wrong way to process the data. Rather, one should look for some related link between the two.

In this example, people drown when they go swimming – when are people most likely to go swimming? The answer, of course, is during the summer. When do people eat ice cream? Ice cream is cold – people eat ice cream when it's hot, and therefore, people eat more ice cream in the summer. Therefore, the cause of both of these is the rise in heat during the summer. This is the causal metric to both of the other two metrics, and it gives a clearer picture of why the two things are related.

One Metric that Matters

In deducing what metrics are most important to you, you're always trying to discover these causal links. For example, if people aren't returning to your site, perhaps the experience isn't enjoyable or useful enough for them to get them to do so. On the other hand, if you have a high amount of people who visit your site but don't register, it could be that they don't find the experience engaging enough. There are a number of different metrics, all of which can give you a different insight into your overall performance as a company.

When you're starting out, you'll want to focus on one of these metrics at any given time. This is referred to as the *one metric that matters*. This concept is really easy to misunderstand. Many people who are newer to the concepts of Lean Analytics actually misinterpret this in a major way and assume that they're only supposed to focus on one thing for the entire duration of the company's run. However, this is *not* the case.

The concept of the one metric that matters basically means that at any given point in your company's growth, there is one metric that you should be focused on changing. You should maintain your focus on changing this metric above all else. This could be anything. For example, if you're at a period where you're trying to generate growth, it might be a good idea to focus solely on a metric relevant to the stickiness of your company and what makes people want to stick around. This could be a metric such as the percentage of unique visitors who come to the site but don't register – this is a number that you want to increase if you're trying to grow as a company and retain users.

What this enables you to do is basically to work on things in such a way that you're able to have absolute focus. You can clearly delineate what you're working on as a company and what all resources need to be aimed at. When you're working with a team, this means that you can focus everybody's productivity on the development of a solution for this given problem. Developing solutions to problems is discussed in the next chapter, which concerns learning.

The idea of the one metric that matters falls into a weird place because it applies to all three phases – the building process, where you're trying to build your product or business to accommodate the metric; the measurement process, where you're obtaining information that correlates to this metric as well as trying to determine what causes this metric; and the learning process, where you review the measurements taken during the previous process to make a reasonable determination on your future action and see what you learned about your user base.

Perhaps the best reason for using the one metric that matters is that it can answer the most important question at any given moment. As a business, and as a startup especially, you're going to be juggling a huge amount of questions and responsibilities. However, the one metric that matters gives you the ability to focus all of these questions and responsibilities toward something that matters the most to your company at that moment. For example, if something is off-balance at your company or there's a particularly nagging question regarding the company in general, that off-balance trait or that nagging question will lead you toward the metric that you need to be studying right then.

Don't be confused like others might – this metric most certainly will change, and knowing which metrics to focus on the most at any given moment is an integral part of growing as an entrepreneur. Once your company gets to be sufficiently large, you *will* have the resources to focus on multiple metrics at once, but until your company gets to that point – and you'll know when it's at that point – you'll have more experience under your belt to direct such a thing.

Another reason this is fantastic is that by understanding what metrics to focus on, you can move through the build-measure-learn process more often. The goal when using Lean Analytics is to go through this cycle as much as possible to force innovation within your product or your company and increment it into the ideal market fit as quickly as possible, i.e., get it to the point where the most people want it and want to use it as quickly as possible.

So, in pursuing this, the concept of focusing on one metric at a time allows you to have a defined metric to try to change, and thereby, to perform experiments on. And that's where we hit one of the most critical parts of this whole thing.

The fact is that not every solution for and increment to your product or business are going to be winners. Not everyone is going to like every change, and not everybody is going to like your company from the get-go either. You have to accept this right now because this is just the truth. However, with all of that said, you need to recognize also that experimentation is a critical part of any business, and it's through experimentation that you start to develop a very good intuition for business and how you grow your company.

Being successful without experiencing failure is called luck – a person couldn't actively replicate it. On the other hand, being successful *with* failure, that's expected – that's the process – and called learning. Learning happens through repeated failures that teach you how to succeed. Remember this as you push forward, especially on to the experimentation part in the following chapter.

Chapter 5: Lean Analytics and the Learn Phase

In some ways, it's more important to explain the learning phase than the measuring phase because, in many ways, the measuring phase happens without your intervention. For example, the analytics programs and suites that you set up will handle a lot of the data gathering *for you*, meaning that you almost never need to even lay a finger on the data until you reach the learning phase, which is where you actually review everything.

The learning phase will change depending on what your company is doing and is *trying* to do in general. For example, if you just ran an experiment during your build phase and then measured it in your measure phase, your learning phase will largely consist of reviewing the results of the experiment both in an isolated sense as well as in regards to the entire business and the business-wide influences that you can enact using that sort of data.

Regardless, this chapter is concerned with the review of that data and with the design of the experiments in response to that data. You're going to be learning what to make of different metrics, as well as how to apply what you learn from those metrics to the broader set of data that you must work with.

Cohort Analysis

The first thing discussed is one very useful way of reviewing the data you've gathered. This is referred to as cohort analysis, and Google Analytics specifically makes it extremely easy to judge cohorts specifically by date of acquisition, i.e., when the users first accessed the site. Other analytics tools offer more ways to keep up with this sort of vital information as well, so keep an eye out for those.

Cohort analysis is when you break down the users accessing a site by different arbitrary categories that you describe. These could be things such as (in the example provided) when they first accessed the site or things like the manner in which they got to the site – if they're users who click on ads or users who haven't engaged with the site in a while.

	Week 1	Week 2	Week 3	Week 4	Week 5	Week 6	Week 7	Week 8	Week 9	Week 10	Week 11
All Users	4.58%	3.08%	2.55%	3.53%	7.25%	4.14%	3.11%	2.22%	2.60%	0.90%	2.94%
Apr 2, 2017 - Apr 8, 2017	0.00%	0.00%	0.00%	0.00%	0.00%	0.00%	0.00%	0.00%	0.00%	0.00%	0.00%
Apr 9, 2017 - Apr 15, 2017	50.00%	44.12%				8.82%	5.88%	2.94%	2.94%	2.94%	2.94%
Apr 16, 2017 - Apr 22, 2017		4.00%	1.30%	2.60%	0.00%	1.30%	0.00%	2.60%	0.00%	0.00%	
Apr 23, 2017 - Apr 29, 2017			7.50%	7.50%		5.00%	5.62%	4.37%	4.37%		
Apr 30, 2017 - May 6, 2017			4.00%		5.75%	2.87%	2.87%	0.57%			
May 7, 2017 - May 13, 2017		2.52%	0.40%	4.50%	4.93%	4.00%	2.11%				
May 14, 2017 - May 20, 2017	12.31%			12.31%	14.62%	9.28%					
May 21, 2017 - May 27, 2017	11.00%	15.36%	3.83%	3.83%	11.50%						
May 28, 2017 - Jun 3, 2017	3.00%	0.00%	3.00%	4.51%							
Jun 4, 2017 - Jun 10, 2017	5.36%	1.44%	0.00%								
Jun 11, 2017 - Jun 17, 2017	3.63%	0.96%									
Jun 18, 2017 - Jun 24, 2017											

This is specifically useful because metrics can be deceptive. For example, let's say that you ran a specific advertising campaign that brought the metrics of your site up. This is great news. However, you then realize that a lot of the new users aren't actually sticking around for a very long time. What could this mean?

Through cohort analysis, you can analyze which users came from where, or when the date of acquisition for users is in comparison to your current ad campaigns, and this will allow you to make logical deductions about the said information. For example, in the case prior, you might have noticed that the user drop-off started after you ran the last ad campaign. The natural conclusion is that perhaps you didn't target the ads correctly and ended up aiming them at people who weren't actually interested in the services you had to offer.

Users divided by various sorts of information are referred to as *cohorts*. Cohorts grouped together by some common elements are referred to as *segments*. You can find quite a bit of information through analyzing how different segments are interacting with your site in particular, and through this, you can figure out where the site may need to up its game as well.

Experiment

One of the most critical parts of the whole experience of build-measure-learn is the experimentation process. Remember, any time that you collect data and then try to assume how to make a change to that data based on an educated guess, you are performing what, for all intents and purposes, amounts to as an experiment. The Lean Analytics model is separated from the traditional model by this fact alone – it is *experiment*-based. The Lean Analytics model aims to scientifically and methodically produce the best company possible while reducing waste and unneeded expenditures as much as it could. In this way, Lean Analytics takes a far more scientific approach to building a business than the typical approach. Because of this, it aims to reduce the sad fact that 75% of startups fail by giving startups the tools for their own success from the very beginning.

This is where we hit one of the most crucial parts of the whole book. You have to be willing to experiment because experimentation implies innovation, and for your site to stay on top of its game, you have to constantly be experimenting and innovating in ways that make your users happy. This isn't to say that you should necessarily try to fix something that isn't broken, but you should have the confidence and the framework in place such that, when the time comes to experiment, you can easily do so. This is a fundamental part of having a company, and it's something you need to respect.

When you analyze your data, remember that you want to figure out the key metric to pay attention to based on the phase your company is in and on any important questions surrounding the company. For example, you may be working on usability and user experience for the site to make it more engaging for visitors and make people more likely to return – all so that you can increase your revenue in the revenue phase thanks to returning users, or so that you can increase the number of users sticking around in the sticky phase. Either way, this gives you a vital base to work with: the metric you need to work on.

You often recognize what your company needs to work on based on the metrics that you observe in the learn phase. At this point, you can start to formulate ideas as to how to make those metrics better by trying to figure out what could cause those metrics to be bad, or what could conversely cause those metrics to start shifting in your favor.

The idea is the first part, and the actual rendering of the idea and the processing of the data from the idea is the second part, which happens when the build-measure-learn cycle repeats once more, in the build cycle.

There are multiple different ways to perform experiments. Let's retrace our steps and look back at trying to improve the user experience to make users more likely to return and use the site, which would improve our revenue as well as our stickiness. You and your team come up with a few different ways to do such a thing, and then you lay them all out. You decide to test all of them and see which one is the best. This is where you sometimes need to think outside the box; sometimes, you can test fundamental ideas without investing much capital or resources into them, or without actually building it – you can do so by simply coming up with a way to measure user response to just the idea.

In any case, at this point, you start coming up with ways to actually work on and hopefully circumvent the problem at hand. One way of doing so in a formulaic way is through the Lean Enterprise Experiment Canvas.

The Lean Enterprise Experiment Canvas is a tool that involves a place where you can list out various things about the problem you've encountered. You can write down the one metric that matters. You can write down the problem from the user's end or the possible problems from the user's end. Afterward, you come up with possible solutions to the problem(s). From here, you also come up with the test for these problems to figure out if the solution is accurate.

BLOOM LEAN ENTERPRISE EXPERIMENT CANVAS		The one metric that matters		Control metric	
Date	Responsible person	Draw a line in the sand: the one metric you want to impact, with how much, by when		If there is a control metric you want to keep an eye on, specify here	
Goal in sure	Project name	Current value of metric		Current value of metric	

Step of cycle		Experiments	1	2	3	4	5
Phrase the problem from your customers' perspective. Include the proof points. Is this really a problem? (validate with clients/data). Is this one of the most important problems? (estimate impact and apply Pareto principle)	Problem						
Define the possible solution. Is the solution easy to implement? Is there a balanced mix of iterative improvements (≥80%) and major leaps (≤20%)?	Solution						
Design the test (I will run experiment #3, with Y% of customers in period Z). Is this the fastest way to test my solution with minimal amount of resources (time, people, money)? Do actual users give feedback, implicitly or explicitly? Is the test time-boxed?	Test method						
Determine what success looks like ("During the test, I expect strong signal from X% of customers/visitors)	Success criterion						
Describe the results of your tests. Based on the results, take a decision.	Result & decision		'Get out of the building'				
Describe the lessons learned from the experiment. Did we change the one metric that matters significantly? Are control variables still ok? If yes, pop champagne, and build the actual solution. If not, post/persevere.	Learning						

Source: LeanAnalyticsBook.com

In defining a test, you want to define a test group and the test that you're going to be running. For example, you might say "I want to implement a chat system, and I'll do so by screening 20% of users for their thoughts on such a thing" or "I want to change the style of the page to make it easier to read, and I'm going to roll out this change for 15% of users to see how differently they respond." This will allow you to come up with a finite group to actually perform your test upon as well as some metrics for how the test will be performed.

Lastly, you want to define what success is in that given experiment. For example, if the user retention rate massively increases due to the style change, or if an overwhelming number of users support a chat system, then that could be seen as a successful experiment which could impact the site positively. Finally, you hit the learning phase, which is basically where you're back to where you are now, and at that point, you're going to review the data and see if your experiment made an impact on your one metric that matters in a profound or important way.

This can raise the question, of course – how do I know what a good experiment is? How do I differentiate a good experiment from a bad experiment? Well, ultimately, what it really comes down to is the amount of resources that would be put into such a thing against how much it's actually expected to change. Since the Lean Analytics system rewards small incremental change in many ways, you most likely want to avoid making massive changes to your overall service that will lead to the waste of your resources over an extended period of time when they could be used for smaller changes that may impact your metrics every bit as much.

In essence, it's not always easy to know what is and isn't a good experiment. It does become easier with time, especially as you start to grasp the core concepts at the very heart of Lean Analytics, but until that point, it can be difficult to really understand. You're just looking for the experiments that have the most potential to impact the one metric that matters the most while also taking the least amount of resources.

Experimentation Using Pre-Existing Data

Let's say that you already have a set of data that you want to work with and you want to run experiments based off of that data to come up with some sort of meaningful conclusions. You can actually do so quite easily. Many of the experiments that you can do with data you already have are similar to the experiments that you perform with data that you collect. You are just looking for key metrics that you want to change and then trying to come up with ways to change that data. Easy!

You also can use the same set of data to try multiple experiments. This is actually good practice in some cases because it allows you to test out multiple different possible conclusions, for the reason that a given metric is down or experiencing a certain change. The process remains much the same, and the difference in experimentation largely comes down to you.

Problem-Solution Canvas

You can also use the problem-solution canvas to come up with meaningful experiments. The problem-solution canvas is designed to help you come up with ways you can fix various issues in your company. Its purpose is to help you convert a problem into a solution with ease.

In the problem-solution canvas, what you essentially do is start out with a description of your customer segment and your customers' problems. In the course of it, you also seek out the root cause of the problem and the various elements of the problem.

For example: you're trying to define the customer segments that the problem affects; you're trying to define what the problem is; you're trying to define what it does to the customer in terms of how they act as well as their emotions before and after the problem; you're trying to define any and all solutions to the problem, anything which limits the customer in question (as in how much they have to spend); you're trying to define the way that the problem behaves; and you're trying to define the way that the problem iterates, the root problem, and the end solution to the problem, in that order.

Of course, the problem-solution fit will vary in its implementation depending on what you're trying to do with it. You might be your own customer, for instance. But using the problem-solution fit, you're trying to work through the problem step by step to come up with a reasonable solution to the problem.

Source: Daria Nepriakhina

Closing

Using these tools, you'll have a clear-cut method for making your way through the learning phase and deducing the useful information from the data that you have. You'll also have a solid framework for coming up with the experiments that you want to carry out in the future.

Chapter 6: Revenue and Calculations

The purpose of revenue is clear: to generate a solid stream of income from small things in your company that isn't necessarily what you're trying to sell – although revenue also encapsulates the things you are trying to sell as well. This means that any money which comes from your site can be considered revenue. The goal of the person starting the business is often to generate as much revenue as they possibly can.

There is a careful line to walk when you're discussing the concept of revenue, however, because it's really easy to try to do too much when it comes to its generation. This is a careful psychological line to walk in and of itself: you don't want your customers to feel like they're just there to make money for you. You want to build a thriving site with a vibrant user base and a lot of things happening – that is how you start to make a site that people want to visit and enjoy.

This chapter involves a lot of general calculations and discussion that would have broken the flow of other chapters, but that is still extremely important to address to have an in-depth knowledge of the concepts covered in this book. For example, things like the viral coefficient and the viral cycle will be covered and what they mean for you regarding Lean Analytics.

Let's start with a discussion of the different types of revenue that different businesses are more likely to want to focus on generating. Note that in the revenue phase, your focus is mostly going to land on the development of mechanisms for the furthering of revenue generation.

People who have marketplace sites are mostly going to generate their money from transactions. There are two different types of marketplace sites, as discussed. On the eCommerce sites, you're going to want to generate a lot of your revenue through user transactions which occur on the site. You're also going to want to try to generate as much customer lifetime value as you possibly can. Two-sided marketplaces are going to generate revenue largely through commission by way of transactions that occur on the site. Rarely do the sites charge transactions at all.

People who have Software as Service sites or mobile apps aimed at users are going to primarily be drawing their revenue through the users on their site. So essentially, whenever users are active on the site, it generates revenue that you can use. This can be calculated through things like customer lifetime value and the customer acquisition cost. You generate revenue through things such as ads and the user's engagement overall. You can also generate it through upselling, which is when you sell products that are of greater value to people already buying or using your services.

The last two types of businesses, featuring user-generated content and media, generate revenue primarily through ads, donations, and similar metrics. Additionally, if you're doing a media-based site, such as a review site, you can get money through cost-per-click advertising services, affiliate marketing, and anything else of that same nature.

All of this is examined a bit more in-depth in the following sections.

Advertising and Revenue

Advertising revenue can take many different forms and is the primary engine by which sites that feature content and media make much of their revenue. Most often, you will generate revenue by hosting things like Google AdSense and related campaigns. You can also generate revenue through things such as cost-per-click advertisements.

One somewhat unrelated form of advertisement is affiliate marketing. Affiliate marketing works extremely well on media-based sites because you can integrate it into your media with ease. Essentially, affiliate marketing is when you act as somebody else's affiliate and advertise their products. Whenever you make a sale – or, depending on the site, whenever you get somebody to view their products – you make a percentage of the sale or a certain amount of money for every view that you get.

Affiliate marketing is a fantastic way to make a fair amount of money regularly, and it scales up based on how popular your site is. If you are interested in affiliate marketing, then you can go to sites such as JvZoo to find affiliates who are looking for people to market their products. These are the companies that you want to talk to and work for. Additionally, many affiliate marketing sites have terms which are very agreeable to the people who are doing the marketing for the site.

Freemium

One common form of revenue generation is the freemium model. The freemium model is defined as a model wherein the initial application, or the application in its simplest form is provided absolutely free to the user. However, additional services are provided to the user at a greater cost. These services may be things which expand the application and the software, or they could be things which lead the software to be more enjoyable in general for the end user.

Mobile games frequently use a freemium model and allow users to spend real currency on things which make the gameplay experience better. This is often a mobile game's primary source of income if they decide to eschew conventional advertisements on the site.

Freemium can be a good or bad thing for your company. On the one hand, if your product is sufficient on its own and the features are just quality-of-life additions, it may not actually generate a whole lot of revenue. Dedicated end users looking for additional features, of course, will opt for the additional features. However, the average user most likely will not. To make up for this, you could price the features higher so that the smaller amount of people buying them makes up for the lost cost since it's highly likely that these people are willing to pay more for said features.

On the other hand, if you decide to make your product difficult to use without buying the additional features, it is likely that hopeful users will stop using the product altogether, feeling ripped off or like they wasted their time downloading something free, and you may suffer significant levels of churn in your company. This is also not very desirable, of course. The best course of action is to only use freemium in cases where it has clear implementations, such as in products that have a significant amount of skill dividing power users and regular users, like video editors. In other cases, it's likely more profitable and wiser to use other models. The only time freemium works significantly well is on mobile apps. Even then, just because the market allows for freemium models doesn't necessarily mean that this kind of model is the best way to go. Even for mobile apps, I would only recommend that you use the freemium model for things that have a significantly large skill gap between the most advanced and the least advanced users.

Paywall

Many sites will opt to use a paywall. This is an incredibly common form of generating revenue amongst sites for things such as newspapers. With a paywall, you allow a user to consume a certain amount of the content that you have available on the site. After they have consumed that much content, you then request that they subscribe to your site. This is a good way to get people to enjoy your site and approach it while also getting them addicted to your content. Once they're in and enjoying your content, they'll most likely want to cross over your paywall and become a subscriber.

Paywalls also exist similarly for things like applications, which will often be passed off as demos for people to get a taste of the application before they go forward with it and decide that they want to buy it. The idea is fundamentally similar: let people try it and become invested in it. Once they're invested in it, they're far more likely to be willing to put their hard-earned cash into the table.

Measuring Value of Customers

This section measures several different things that are particularly useful in making value determinations regarding users. There are a few different metrics that will be covered and defined to understand what they mean in context.

The first is how one can determine the lifetime value of a customer. This metric is valuable for developing an idea of what your customers are worth and how much they're worth in the long-term. This is one of those cases where it's particularly useful and easy to use Google Analytics to gather the relevant information.

Customer lifetime value is essentially a calculation of how much a customer generates over the entire course of the time that they are your customer. This is how much they've generated from their first purchase all the way up to their last purchase.

People who enjoy your shop or your website will return many times and will try to keep shopping at your website. They will order multiple things and generate quite a lot of revenue. Whatever you spend to acquire these customers – whether through advertising campaigns, virality, or anything of the like – will benefit you each time the customer returns and starts to generate even more revenue than they did before. Therefore, when more customers spend more money, the customer lifetime value goes up. Customer lifetime value, when calculated, is basically how much you can expect a customer to spend at your company over the period that the person buys things from your company.

There is no standard method to find the average customer lifetime value. There are a bunch of different models that you can use, and some are simpler than others. For current purposes, let's calculate the lifetime value of customers as *the average profit of each order multiplied by the average amount of orders each customer places.* You can also subtract the average cost of your advertising campaigns to get an estimate of how much you're spending on each customer.

The point of the average customer lifetime value is to give you an idea of how much you can spend to acquire future customers without losing profit. The goal is to break even. So if your average customer had a lifetime value of $120 after the average of your advertising campaigns was subtracted, you can assume that you can spend $120 on every future customer acquisition without losing any money on them.

Another thing that you need to pay attention to is the cost to acquire customer or *CAC*. This is how much it costs to acquire a given customer. You can figure out what this is by dividing how much you spent getting more customers – that is, how much you spent on the marketing practices of the company such as advertisements and placements – by the number of customers that you acquired.

Let's say, for example, that you spent $150 on marketing in the year 2016, and that same year you gained 300 customers. You would have a CAC of about $2, meaning that each customer costs you about $2 to acquire based on your current marketing tactic.

In Lean Analytics, the former two metrics are actually really powerful. First, they give you a vantage of how people are viewing your site. For example, if your CAC is particularly high, then you might be drastically mistargeting your ads. You might need to do a cohort analysis to determine where your campaigns are falling short and which campaigns aren't meaningfully converting people into customers. You can assume that people are customers if, in lieu of a better measure, they come to your site many times. You can also most likely determine who is spending money on your site through IP addresses and figure out which people are customers and which people aren't. Many analytics engines and storefront APIs will offer this sort of functionality in a very simple setting that will make it easy to process this sort of vital information.

Additionally, these are important parts of building revenue in certain kinds of sites, especially if those sites depend on advertising or the like to make revenue. "Customer" can be very vaguely defined and can also be described as the amount that is spent to gain *users*. In this case, on a site with mandatory advertising such as YouTube, you can gain a lot of money by making your site have a lower CAC because the implication is that you can get more people for less money, who in turn generate revenue through the advertisements on your site.

Measuring Value of Users and Visitors

The previous section's last paragraph explained in brief why consistently valuating your users could be particularly useful. This section will go into more detail about valuating your users and your site's visitors.

The lifetime value of users – particularly in sites where they aren't expected to buy items and are instead expected to generate revenue through given channels such as advertising or affiliate marketing – can be useful to calculate. It is also calculated very similarly to the lifetime value of customers. Firstly, you look at the total revenue generated. Then you divide it by the number of users that you have each month. There are times when it's not clear-cut, however, because you also have to account for the average of your advertising campaigns to determine, on average, how much it cost to *get* these users. What you end up with is the average lifetime value of a singular user, or how much a single user has generated for you. This can be a great metric because it tells you how much users make and what you can expect of them in particular as you go forward.

You're trying to increase the lifetime value of your users by lowering the amount spent to get them and by increasing the amount of revenue that they generate (e.g., better affiliate marketing plugs, better ad targeting on your own site, and so forth). More lifetime value per user obviously indicates that the users themselves are generating more money for you.

You also want to measure the value of visitors. Visitors are people who don't necessarily sign up for your site but who generate value anyway. Many people who use sites such as news sites are simply visitors without accounts, but they still may generate revenue for the sites by viewing advertisements or clicking affiliate marketing links. Much like before, you can determine the value of visitors by dividing the total amount of revenue generated by the site by the number of unique visitors to the site each month. This will give you an idea of how much revenue each visitor is generating.

Viral Coefficient and Viral Cycle

This topic is related because it addresses the concept of virality. In lowering your cost to acquire customers or in increasing your lifetime value of customers and users, you're trying to draw in more people using less money and, thereby, generate more revenue thanks to their presence. Having a solid idea about this concept can help you a lot.

Now, let's talk about the viral coefficient as well as the viral cycle time. These are absolutely essential concepts in the realm of viral marketing, and it's important that you have a firm knowledge of them going forward. Everybody knows that being a viral content means many people are quickly spreading the content through word of mouth. What many people don't take into account is that there is a formulaic way of analyzing viral growth.

Viral growth is called such because it is the manner by which something is spread from user to user. Things, when spread by word of mouth or shared by influential people, can grow at an incredibly fast rate. This rate of growth is referred to as viral growth. Viral growth is an important aspect of marketing because achieving steady viral growth is something that you without a doubt want to do. Viral growth has a few different elements, and one of the most important is the viral coefficient.

Specifically, let's assume that you have an initial set of customers, c. Let's say that each of these customers sends a link to your website to x amount of people. Next, let's say that we have a conversion rate r, which signifies the percentage of people who will actually click the link and sign up.

This means we can assume that for every one person sending out a link to your site or product to x people, $r*x$ of those people will sign up. This gives us our viral coefficient. You can use the viral coefficient to guess how many people each individual person will be able to recruit. This means that given a conversion rate of 30% and everybody sending the link to 20 people, every single person will create 6 new customers (20*6).

Assuming we had an initial customer base of 10 who created 6 new customers each in period 1, this means that at the start of period 2, we can expect that we had 60 customers. This system is a little messy, but it does very easily represent how viral growth in marketing works and how you can make predictions and come up with analytics regarding conversion rates based on how many people your customers recommend the site to against how many people actually sign up for the site. You can use the average of these, or the line of regression over an extended period of time, to estimate how the growth will continue to happen down the line.

Another important aspect to all of this is what is referred to as the *viral cycle time*. The viral cycle time refers to the amount of time it takes for the viral cycle to complete. The viral cycle is essentially defined as follows: customer 1 sees the application, customer 1 tries the application, customer 1 likes the application and decides to invite people, customer 1 invites customer 2, customer 2 opens the application, and the process starts all over again. This is important because the shorter this process is, the faster that viral growth can actually occur.

Subscription-Based Services

The last major source of revenue is subscription-based services. An increasing amount of businesses have been aiming themselves more toward subscription-based services. Even things which used to be released without a subscription such as Microsoft Office have started to move to a subscription-based platform.

It makes sense – it is often more profitable to sell a pretty cheap subscription for something that you know people are going to be continually using, as opposed to selling it with a huge price up front. This has become the go-to selling tactic for things such as Microsoft Office, the Adobe Suite, and much more. Additionally, if you run a media site, offering a subscription to the media that you produce can allow you to have a constant stream of revenue – so long as you can keep the subscribers where they are, of course.

Chapter 7: Breaking Lean Analytics Down Into Stages You Can Follow

To help you see success with Lean Analytics, there are a few stages that you need to be aware of. You can't go on to the following stage if all the steps in the previous one are not completed properly. While you can break Lean Analytics down as much as you would like, there are five main steps that you can focus on to get the work done. These five steps that help you implement lean support methodology will include:

• Stage 1: This is the stage where you will concentrate on finding a problem. There are people out there who are looking for a solution, while you need to find the problem that you can provide a solution to. You will find that a business which focuses its energy on selling between businesses is going to really need to focus on this step. If you find the problem that you want to work on, then it is time to move on to the next step.

• Stage 2: In the second stage, it is your job to create an MVP product that your early customers can try out. In this stage, your primary focus is going to be user engagement and retention. You can also spend some time learning how to make this happen. This requires some experimental steps, and you may even need to go through it and try several products to find out which one is the best for you. You need to get as much response from the customer as possible to help direct you where you should go next.

• Stage 3: Once you have a chance to put your product in the hands of the first few customers, and you get some of their feedbacks of the product, it is time to learn some of the best and most effective ways that you can reach out to more customers. Once you get that plan in place, and new customers start to purchase your product, then you can move on to stage four. Remember that it needs to be cost-efficient here. You can't pick out a product that is popular—but then it makes you go bankrupt because it costs so much to put together and advertise. Make sure that your product is easily adaptable and usable by many customers and that you can make the profits you need to keep growing.

• Stage 4: At this point, it is time to remember some of your old economics classes and focus on how much revenue you will make from selling this product. You want to find ways to optimize your revenue so that you can provide a high-quality product while still making some good profits in the process. To do this, you should calculate out the LTV: CAC ratio. LTV is the amount of revenue that you expect to get from your customer, and the CAC is going to be how much you spent to get that customer.

o You can get your ratio by dividing the LTV by the CA. if you get an LTV that is about three times higher than your CAC, then your margins are in the right place. Of course, the higher your margins are, the better it is for your business because it means you are making some good profits.

• Stage 5: In this stage, you will take the necessary actions to help the business grow. If you are doing well and making a high enough margin, then you would continue on with the current plan. If you are not making a high enough margin, you may want to make some necessary changes so that you can keep your business growing. This is also the time where you would concentrate on what you would like to do in the future. Remember that the main goal for your business at all times is to keep growing and making more revenue. In this step, you will be able to evaluate how your current plan went, and decide if you should keep things the same or change them.

If you are able to keep up with these five steps on all the products that you try to sell to the consumer, then you are going to gain tremendous success. They are simple steps, but ones that a lot of businesses fail to do well with. This is especially true when it comes to the testing of products with your customers before releasing to the market. Make sure to follow down each one when your product is ready, so before you release it, you are going to end up with a successful product that makes you a lot of profit.

Chapter 8: Understanding Metrics and What They Mean to Your Business

One of the things that you need to know when you decide to work with Lean Analytics is that most people are going to use the data they have wrongly. When you gather data, but you don't gather the right data, or you gather it in the wrong way, then you will miss out on important patterns and won't make products that your customers actually want.

There are a lot of false metrics out there. They can make a company feel good because they seem to point to good results. The number of likes that you get on Facebook is a good example of this. You may feel good because you got 100 likes on a post, but these likes don't really tell you much other than the customer saw your post. It doesn't tell you who the customer is, where they are from, whether they purchased the product or not, or how long they spent looking at the post. All it says is that they spent two seconds glancing at it, and then hit a button.

Avoiding these false metrics is so important for the success of Lean Analytics. You don't want to get distracted from what is actually important, which is the information that can actually make your business some money. When you don't go and learn how to use your data right, then you will miss out on opportunities, patterns, and results that you can achieve to further improve your business.

Now, there are going to be two main parts that come with this idea. These include:

o There are many companies and people who will use words like "data-driven." They often use a ton of resources to compile data to look important. But while they are bringing in the data, they are missing out on the driven part. Few are actually going to make a strategy that is based on whatever information they gather from the data. Sure, they may have the right data at their disposal, but they either choose to not respond to that information in the proper way, or they don't understand the data.

o Even if the company makes sure that their actions are data driven, there could be an issue with the metrics going wrong. Often, these companies are going to simplify the metrics too much because they use them according to the convention. You have to remember that just because some people do this, doesn't mean that it is the right way for what you are trying to do. If you don't use the information the right way, then the data going in is going to be garbage and the analysis coming out won't be much better.

As a business that wants to start using Lean Analytics, you have to spend some time learning what a false metric is, and what a meaningful metric for your business is. If you get caught in the trap of following false metrics, then you are going to end up with a strategy that pushes you away from your goals and will waste a lot of your effort and your time.

The false metrics you must look out for

Since your business is working to cut out as many excess expenditures as possible, while still providing a great product and fantastic customer service to your customers, you must be extra careful that you are not using any of the false metrics that are likely to come up. Many people who don't have a good understanding of data and how it works will see these false data points, and assume these are actually what they should listen to. This ends up being a huge waste of your time and talent.

There are a number of false metrics that come up. They may look appealing to you at first, but they often lead you in the wrong direction, when it comes to developing a new strategy for your company. Some of the false metrics that you should watch out for are:

How many hits you get: If your website is really busy and all, it is likely that you are going to get a large number of hits. But this doesn't really show you what the customer is most interested in. It shows that they looked around, but that's about it.

• Page views: The page views will refer to how many pages are clicked on a website during a specific amount of time. If you are going to choose a metric, then this is one to work with, but it is still seen as a waste of time by most. In many cases, unless you are doing some business that depends on the number of page views, such as those who are advertising, then it is better to work with a program that can count how many unique visitors you get each month.

• Number of visitors: While it is a good idea to know how many visitors visit your website, this number is often too broad. For example, when we talk about this metric, are we talking about one person who possibly came to the same site one hundred times, or were there one hundred people who came once? As a business, you are more interested in seeing the second group because it means that more impressions were made and that you probably got more sales.

• Number of likes, friends, or followers: With so many companies moving to online and social media, this false metric is one that they really need to watch out for. This one basically shows you false popularity. A better metric to go with would be the level of influence that you have. What this means is how many people will do what you want them to do? Yes, followers and likes on your Facebook page can be nice, but you should focus more on some other metrics.

• Email addresses: A large email list is a great way to work on your business, but you have to consider how valuable that list is. Just because you can produce a large list, doesn't mean that everyone on that list will open, read, and then act on whatever message you send out. You can have an email list, but you want to make sure that the addresses on it are high quality; even if that means that you have a list that is smaller. If you are in the process of collecting emails, then you should aim to get emails from those who are actually interested in what you have to offer.

• How many downloads you get: This is a metric some companies will use for their downloadable products. Yes, these downloads can help to increase your rankings in the marketplace where you sell them, but this number doesn't give you any meaningful information. If you want to work with some more precise answers, then you need better metrics. For example, looking at the Launch Rate is good because it is going to show you the percentage of those who downloaded, created, an account, and then actually used your product. You can work with something known as Percentage of users who pay to see your profits.

• How much time someone is spending on your website: This is only going to be useful information if your business works with engaged time to make profits. You don't really want to look at this time, because the customer could be spending their time on your page, but not how you want them. If the customer spends time on your complaint page, that's not a good thing for your business, even if it shows that someone spent a lot of time on the website.

If you are looking to pick out some metrics that can actually provide you with good information that will get your business to grow, then you have to avoid the metrics above. They sometimes are appealing and will look good at first glance, but they are basically just giving you information that is useless. Companies who follow these false metrics often end up wasting their time and money and then getting nowhere in the end.

Recognizing and working with good metrics

Now that we have taken a look at false metrics and how they are going to lead your business astray, it is time to look at what metrics count. You want to go with a metric that will move you towards your defined goal, not one that is going to waste a lot of time and money and not produce results. Is this sometimes hard for you to accomplish? As a business, how are you supposed to pick out a good metric that will push you towards your goals?

The good news is that there are a few characteristics of a good metric that you can look for. These will include:

• Comparable: You are working with a good metric if it can be considered comparable. You can ask yourself the following questions to help test whether it meets this requirement:

o How was the metric last year or last month? Is the rate of conversion increasing? A Cohort analysis will help you to track the conversion rate to see about this one.

• Understandable: Any metric that you use needs to be simple and understandable. Everyone who takes a look at the metric should be able to understand what it is. This ensures that the metric isn't so complicated that you get lost when using it.

• Ratio: You are not going to work with absolute numbers when it comes to metrics. If you end up with these absolute numbers, then it is time to make some changes and convert it for easier comparisons. The easier your comparisons are, the easier it is for you to make some sound business decisions.

• Adaptability: If you choose a metric, it will need to change the same way that the business changes. If you see that your metric is moving, but you can't pinpoint where it is going, then this is not a good metric. You want the metric to move with you, rather than randomly—all on its own. If the metric goes off on its own, then you do not have a secure metric to rely on.

With that said, there are two main metric types that you can rely on when you work on Lean Analytics. These are going to be quantitative and qualitative metrics. Qualitative metrics are the ones that will have a direct impact or contact with your customers. This could include metrics like interviews and feedback. This gives you some good information from your customers, which makes it a good metric.

Sometimes you will need to work with a quantitative metric. These are going to be more about the numbers, rather than the quality of your metric. You can use this metric to help you to know which questions you should ask your customer.

Both of these metrics are going to be usable when you are growing your business. They will also have some different types of metrics that fit under them so that you know exactly which one to use. Some of the different metric types that you can use that fit under these two main types include:

▪ Vanity metrics: These are metrics that will have no impact on the behavior of what you are focusing on. They are basically a waste of your time, and you need to learn how to recognize them ahead of time. They sometimes can be tempting to follow because they may seem like they will give you good advice, but they will end up leading you nowhere.

▪ Actionable metrics: These are the metrics that will change the behavior of the thing you focus on. These are the best metrics to work with on a new product. They can lead you straight to the course of action that you want to follow and can sometimes make it easier to pick your strategy.

▪ Reporting metrics: These are the metrics you will use in order to figure out how well your business is doing and if you need to make any changes to become more efficient.

▪ Exploratory metrics: These are the metrics that you can use when you want to find out something new. If you want to learn more about your customers, learn more about a certain process your company is doing, or something similar, you will work with exploratory metrics.

▪ Lagging Metrics: These are good metrics to work on if you want to get a bit of history about your company, and you need as many details as you can possibly get. The churn of your company is a good example of this kind of metric. This is because you will be able to look through and see how many customers ended up canceling their orders in the last year, or however long you want to look back on.

▪ Leading metrics: You can work with leading metrics sometimes because they will provide you with some information to help forecast your business. A good leading metric could be some of the complaints from your customers because they give you a good idea of what the customer wants and how they are going to react to something in the future.

During your Lean Analytics process, you must determine the metrics you want to use. The ones that you pick can sometimes be based on which product or problem you are working on at that moment. Often, it is best to just work on one metric, at least at a time, because this makes it easier for you to keep track of things and not get the information confused. All of these metrics can be nice, as long as you use them properly and know how to accurately read the information that they give back.

Chapter 9: Analytical Tests to Use with Lean Analytics

There are a wide variety of tests that you can work on when it comes to Lean Analytics. These are meant to help you examine any of the assumptions that you may want to use. You can use them to help you learn more about the customer feedback you get so that you can respond to your customers accordingly. Let's take a look at a few of the most popular analytical tools that you can choose so that you can start to use them in your own Lean Analytics project.

Segmentation

Segmentation is the first test that we are going to look at. The process of segmentation is to compare your data from a large demography. Often, your customers are going to come from a large set of demographics. There will be different ages, different genders, different wants and needs, and even different locations—where they live, and where they work. Looking at all the customers as a whole can be tiring and can lead you to be confused. You can use segmentation to divide up your demographics in any manner that you choose.

Depending on the project you want to work on, you may have a specific way to divide up your demographics. You may want to do it by where the customers live, their age, their lifestyle, their income group, and even their gender. This can help you to better look through your customers, and also to find out where people are purchasing your product, if there are some different buying styles between male and female customers, or if there seems to be an age group that fits most of your customer base.

The reason that you want to make your own user segments is that this ensures that the data you have, can become actionable. Analytics can give you a ton of information about those who are purchasing products from you, but sometimes the information is just too much and too vast. This makes it hard for you to draw some good conclusions from the information. After all, while gathering the information that you have received in the past can be a good thing; although, it isn't always the best way to help improve your conversion rate or retention.

This is where the process of segmentation is going to come into play. When you learn how to filter out the audience, you will then be able to create a better plan to make new products that serve them the most. Analytics can give you the information that you need, but segmentation can help you act on it.

For example, you may have a conversion rate that seems average or good, but it could be from a combination of one group that converts really high and consistently, and then another group that seems to never convert at all. You could be wasting a lot of money on that second group where you are hardly getting anybody to convert at all. Segmentation can be used to help you understand what things you are doing the right way—when engaging the first group, and can give you a plan on how you can improve to work on that second group.

When you are working on segmentation, you don't want to just focus on the data so that you can learn about the users. This isn't just a history project. You also want to focus on that data so that you can find something to act upon. Segmentation is one of the best ways to do this. You can take your customer base and the information that you have on them, and then divide it up based on certain criteria. From here, you can learn what steps you should take to advertise and reach your customers—and more like them—to increase profits.

The important thing here is to remember that not all of the customers you encounter are going to be the same. It is possible that some of the customers in your database will purchase something once, and then not come back. It isn't a bad thing to reach out to those customers because you may entice them to make another purchase. But you really want to figure out who your regular audience is. You want to know what they best respond to, and how you can keep them coming back for more. This will help you to grow your business and earn more in profits over the years.

So, the next question you may have is how do you create a good segment of your customers? There are a lot of options here to help you. The best thing to do is take a look at the process that you can use to help create segmentation for your Lean Analytics projects. The steps include:

Define what the purpose of segmenting is: The first step is to figure out how you want to use this segmentation. Do you want to use it to gain more customers? Do you want to use this information to better manage a portfolio for your current customers? Do you want to be able to reduce waste, be more efficient, or do you have something else in mind? Taking the time to define your purpose makes it easier to know the steps to segment out your customers.

Decide which variables are important to you: These will really influence the purpose of this process. Take out some paper and list them in order of how important they are. You can list them out in a Clustering or in a Decision Tree. For example, if you want to do a segmentation to figure out which of your products are the most popular and bring in the most money, then you would need to set out parameters like cost and revenue.

Once you have these variables in place, it is time to list out the granularity and the threshold of creating your segments. You will need to end up with two or three levels for every variable that you pick. Sometimes you may need to adapt this. Some problems that are more complex may need more levels for the variables.

Assign your customers to each cell. This can give you a clear picture of whether there is a fair distribution present or not. If you end up not seeing this distribution, then it is time to figure out why. You may need to make some tweaks to your thresholds to make this all work. Keep tweaking this information until your distributions are fair.

Include your segmentation in your analysis. You can then spend some time checking it out and seeing what information you are able to get from it.

Cohort Analysis

The next test that you can try out is known as a Cohort Analysis. This is where you are going to use a time bucket in order to compare a few sets of data. With this one, there are going to be differences in behavior between the customers who showed up to get the free trial of your product, the ones who were there at the initial launch, and those who show up when you enter the full payment stage.

Each of these stages is important because it will help you figure out which customers are the most likely to come back and be repeat customers as your company grows. The customers who show up during the first two stages, especially the free trial, are probably not the most serious customers and ones you won't want to spend a lot of time on. These may include some customers who just wished to try out the product and didn't want to invest in it beyond trying it out.

Those who show up after the first two stages are better customers to concentrate on. These are the customers who will really be interested in the product, because they put some investment into it, some money to get the product. You will need to study the customers in these two stages with the help of your cohort analysis to help you learn more about your true customer base and how they behave. This will give you some valuable information to help you market to these individuals later on.

A/B Tests

The next type of test that you can do in Lean Analytics is A/B testing. This is a process that you can use in order to examine an attribute between your two choices. It could be something as simple as a slogan, image, or color. You would do this test in order to determine which option is the most effective.

An example of this is that you have two products that you want to compare to see which one your customers will respond to. You would run this test and then use the information you gather to figure out why they chose one product over the other.

To get this test to really work well, you must make sure that you only switch out one thing on the product. You can't submit two completely different products to the customers and expect this test to work. You will get varying results, and you won't be able to tell what to fix. So, let's say that you are working on a website. You would have one version that has a red background, and then the other version would have a blue background. You could then work with the A/B testing to determine which one your customers liked the best, or responded to the most, out of those choices. Outside of the background color, everything else must stay the same for this test to work.

The most effective A/B testing is going to be where there is only one attribute that is different. Then you can easily make decisions based on what the customer likes or doesn't like. In some cases though, you would work with multivariate analysis. This is where you will go through and compare several changes against another group of changes so that you can tell the one that is the most effective.

There are going to be a few key things that you must have in place to make sure that you can properly do your A/B test. These are:

o You must have a great idea for running the A/B test. You need to know your reason before you even get started.
o Whatever item that you want to test must be noticeable to the audience. If you try to make a minor change that no one will really notice, then you will not get reliable results.

o It is best if you are able to just test one of your variables at a time. If you work on multivariate testing, you could run into the issue of not really knowing what variable is the one that customers like or dislike.

o Your test should be statistically significant. This means that your sample size should be large enough so that you know that your results are pretty valid with some margin of error.

To help you understand how the A/B testing is going to work, we need to take a look at an example. We will use this kind of testing on a website that your company is looking to improve. There are two ways that you can try to do this, and they are:

o You will test out the pages with separate pages for each one

o You will work with some JavaScript code to conduct a test that happens inside the page. This is nice because you won't have to work with two separate URLs to make it work

With the first option, you will have to create two different URLs for the two pages that you would like to test out. You can give them names that are similar, but you should change them enough so that you are able to keep track of them without getting too confused.

If you want to go with the second option, you have to have some experience with coding and with JavaScript. You would then need to place some code on your website to ensure that it can dynamically serve one option or the other.

The method out of these two that you decide to go with is going to depend on your personal preferences and the tools that you are going to rely on. Both of these testing results will provide you with good and valid results, but they are going to take different amount of times to set up and to implement.

Testing processes are important when it comes to how well your company will do. They will ensure that you are creating a product that your customer really wants, rather than just working on a product and hoping that it turns out fine in the market. The testing that you choose to go with is going to depend on what works for your product and for your industry.

Chapter 10: The Lean Analytics Cycle

Before you decide to work with the Lean Analytics methodology, it is important that you know a little more about the cycle that comes with it. This cycle is going to ensure that you stay on the right track when you get started, and will help you to get the most out of this methodology. There are four important steps that come with this process and making sure that that you make this process work for you.

A good way that you can think about this Lean Analytics Cycle is similar to the scientific method. You will need to go through the whole process like the scientific method, such as determining what you need to do to improve your business, forming your hypothesis to lead to a discovery, and then work on an experiment to see if your hypothesis will work. And if the hypothesis is wrong, then you don't give up. You keep trying new experiments, even changing the hypothesis if needed, until you find the solution that is right.

This Lean Analytics Cycle is a great way to keep track of what needs to be done when developing a new product or changing up a process that your business follows. Let's take a closer look at these steps, the scientific method of the business world so that you can use the Lean Analytics Cycle.

What should I improve?

The first question we are going to look at in the Lean Analytics Cycle is to understand what you must improve in your business. Remember that the job of this cycle is not to teach you something new about the business. If you are relying on this cycle to teach you something new, then you are going to be disappointed. You must already be knowledgeable about all the aspects of your business, and you should have a good idea of what you would like to work on to improve your business.

In this first step, you may find that it is beneficial to talk to some other business peers to discuss which metric you should use. The cycle can help you figure out the most relevant metric that will work for your business in the here and now. You could also use some information from your business model to figure out the right metric as well.

After you have chosen which metric you want to use, you will then need to connect that metric back to the Key Performance Indicator. A good example of this is a metric that is used as the conversion rate if the KPI is the amount of people who will already purchase your product.

To help you make this step a bit easier to work with, you will want to sit down and think of all the possible metrics that you could work with. Think of three that you already use in your business or that you think are important for the business. Then right next to these metrics, you can write down which KPI you would measure for each metric. This will give you a good place to start.

Form your hypothesis

This is a stage where some creativity needs to come into play. The hypothesis is going to give you the answers that you need to move forward. You will need to look for inspiration here, but you can find it in one of two ways. You can look for an answer for something like "If I perform ___, I believe ____ will happen, and ____ will be the outcome."

You will need to check through the data that you have available to help you answer these questions. You will be surprised at how easily you can find any answers you need if you actually read through your data. If you, for some reason, don't have data at all, you may need to get started on collecting this data so that you have a place to start. You can consider some of the strategies that your competitors use, follow practices that seemed to have worked well for businesses that are similar to yours, work on surveys, or study the market for your industry to see what your options will be for this step.

The most important thing that you are going to work on in this step is that when you are working with the hypothesis, it is there to point you in the direction of thinking like your audience. You will want to keep asking questions until you understand what the audience is thinking. It can also work to help you understand how your customer or your audience will behave or react to your product, service, or the changes you plan to make.

Conduct your experiment

Once your hypothesis is written out, you will then need to work on an experiment that will test it out. To help you get started on that, there are three main questions that you can consider so that you conduct the experiment in the proper way. These three questions include:

o Who is your target audience? You must take some time to think about your customer and whether they are actually the right customers for your business. Could you get better results, or more sales, if you worked with a different target audience? Even if your current audience is good, are there better ways that you could reach out to them compared to how you reach out to them right now?

o What are you expecting your current target audience to do? It would often be that you want them to purchase your product. You need to check to make sure if your audience can easily understand what you want them to do. And you want to make sure that the action is as easy to do as possible. For example, if you want your audience to go purchase the product online, and your website is hard to find, or the purchase button doesn't work, then you are reducing your sales because it becomes too hard. You should also check to see how many of your target audience who sees your message actually complete your desired task.

o Consider why you think that the audience should do the action? Have you provided them with the right motivation? Do you think that your current strategy is doing the job? If you find that your target audience isn't motivated for you, are they showing motivation for your competitor instead?

These questions should be answered ahead of time because they are a great tool when it comes to understanding your customer better. Working on which experiment you will do at this stage doesn't have to be difficult, you can simply use the sentence below to help guide you in the right direction to get started with it:

"WHO will do WHAT because WHY to improve your KPI towards the defined goals or target."

If you have already gone through the previous steps and picked out a good hypothesis, then you won't find that it is too hard for you to go and come up with a good experiment that you can try as well. Once you have your experiment in place, you can go and set up the Lean Analytics to help you measure the KPI and finish up with your chosen experiment.

Measure the outcomes and then decide what to do next

It isn't going to do your business a lot of good to start out with a new experiment and then walk away from it. You need to be able to measure how well it goes, and what results you get from the work, to determine if it is working the way that you want. And if the experiment doesn't end up doing what you want, then you have to decide if you can make some small changes to make it work, or if it is time to restart and work from scratch.

Here, you are also able to make a decision on what steps you should take next based on the results that you get out of your experiments. There are a few things that you should really look for and pay attention to when you are measuring the outcomes during this final stage. Those things are:

• Would you consider your experiment to be successful? If you do, then your metric would be done. You would then be able to implement the experiment on a regular basis and then move on to finding the next issue and metric that you need to work on with your business.

• Did the experiment end up failing? Then it may be time to revise the hypothesis that you came up with. You should stop here and try to think about why the experiment failed or why it didn't work the way that you wanted it to. This can help you make a better hypothesis the next time around.

• Did the experiment move a bit, but it did not end up reaching your defined goal? This is where you may not need to change the hypothesis, but you do need to go and define a new experiment. If you think that your hypothesis is still a viable one, then it is fine to stay with it, but you do need to make some changes to the experiment that you are working with.

Depending on the type of project that you work on, there may be many iterations of the experiment before you are done. It is likely that you will test out the hypothesis several different times. You may even need to scratch the hypothesis that you are working with a few times, in order to pick out something better. The trick here is to keep on working towards it until you come up with a solution that is efficient, will work for your business, and will make your customers happy. Once you reach that goal, then you will be ready to implement it and move on to working on the next metric for your company.

The Lean Analytics Cycle is not meant to be something that is complicated or hard to learn. It is meant to be a simple solution that you can follow in order to help your business and grow it more than before. If you have worked with the scientific method in the past, then you can just implement the stages that you previously worked on, in order to come up with the solutions that your business needs.

Conclusion

Thank you for making it to the end of *Lean Analytics: The Ultimate Guide to an Agile Way of Analytics, Advanced Analytics, and Data Science for a Superior Way to Build Startups and Run Enterprises*. It should have been informative and provided you with all of the tools you need to achieve your goals, whatever they may be.

The next step is to start applying what you've learned. The simple nature of Lean Analytics makes it really easy to start a business even if you don't have a huge amount of resources. This makes it a great tool for low-budget entrepreneurs. It also means that there is almost no reason for you to hold back and avoid using Lean Analytics to make more money. At this point, it's just about you taking the necessary steps forward and trying to implement these ideas in your business.

Finally, if you found this book useful in any way, a review on Amazon is always appreciated!

Check out more books by James Edge

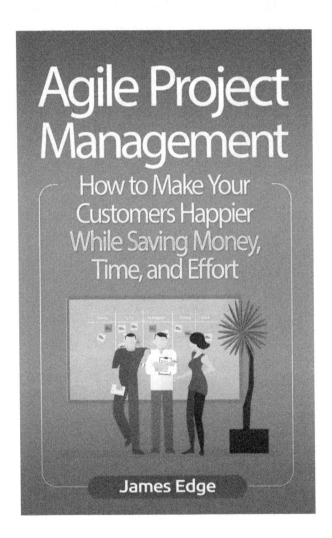

Made in the
USA
Middletown, DE